Investing

A Comprehensive Guide To Gaining Financial
Independence And Managing Your Budget: A
Comprehensive Guide To Gaining Financial
Independence And Managing Your Budget

*(This Book Provides A Comprehensive Understanding Of
Investments)*

Fredrick Murillo

TABLE OF CONTENT

Additional Terms In The Trading Of Options

Options that are eligible for trading on a national trading platform, such as the Chicago Board Options Exchange or CBOE, are referred to as listed options. Typically, a listed option is equivalent to 100 shares of a specific stock. A 100-share option of this kind is also called a single contract. Every contract has set strike prices and expiration dates.

When the share price of a call option surpasses the strike price, it is considered to be in the money. On the other side,

The premium is the cost of any choice, expressed as its total price. Numerous things influence it, such as stock price, strike price, time value, and volatility.

Contract names: Like stock ticker symbols, options contracts can have names or logos that are comparable to them.

Ask price: This is the amount that a seller is willing to take as payment for trading the option. In essence, this would be the premium you would have to pay if you wanted to buy votes.

Volume: The total number of contracts exchanged in a single day is referred to here.

Change: The price difference between the prior and current trading periods is referred to here. A percentage is sometimes used to signify change.

The simple measurement of a stock's price fluctuation between its daily high and low is called volatility. Volatility has long been calculated from historical data.

Implied volatility, or IV, is a metric that quantifies the probability that a market believes a stock will see a large price swing. Some of these factors can be measured with specific instruments. Among them is Vega. The Vega pricing model computes the theoretical impact of a single-point shift in implied volatility.

Given the possible upside for the options contract, high implied volatility indicates high options prices. It is wise to remember that measurements of volatility are never precise; they are merely guesses. Most of them are forecasts for the anticipated shift in an option's price.

Employee stock options are a kind of call option, albeit they are not easily accessible to all traders. In an effort to keep their valued and skilled employees—especially the management—on board for an extended length of time, many publicly traded corporations provide stock options to them.

Employee stock options are quite similar to regular stock options in that holders are granted the right, but not the responsibility,But the contract is exclusive to the arrangement between an employee and the company's owners or board. It cannot be exchanged or traded by others on the options stock markets.

However, if the selections are listed, then this is different. A listed option represents a contract between two distinct parties. This contract can be readily traded on the markets and has no connection to the company at all.

Mutual Funds with Dividend Payments

A plethora of organisations offer mutual funds that specialise in dividend investments. This enables you to receive dividend income in addition to having a diversified investment portfolio. Keep in mind that dividends from mutual funds are not qualifying. This implies that you will need to regard the income from mutual fund dividend distributions as regular income.

Allow us to examine a few instances. The DRIPX fund is one dividend-paying fund. It makes investments in businesses that provide dividend reinvestment plans, or DRIPS, as you may remember. Consequently, the fund will reinvest its dividends. After ten years, the yield was 13%, and the return was 1.75%.

The Vanguard International High Dividend Yield Index Fund is known as VIHIX. This fund makes investments in foreign businesses in an effort to make money. It searches for slowly expanding firms with high dividend yields. It will bring in the cash right now. This fund has a low expense ratio and a respectable 4% yield.

Mutual Funds: The final word

Mutual funds may be an alternative for individuals who prefer that someone else manage their finances. But if you're reading this book, you likely want to get more involved in your investment. It's a good idea to avoid using mutual funds, even if that's your inclination. With the exception of having a professional fund manager, exchange-traded funds offer nearly all of the same advantages. The true value of having an experienced fund manager is still being determined. First off, it's debatable if they outperform passively managed funds like exchange-traded funds in terms of beating the market. You are also required to cover any costs related to the loading and fees. Dividend investing should be viewed as starting your own business. You will want to reduce your spending as much as you can in light of this. So, since you don't have to, why pay exorbitant load fees?

When examining several mutual funds, it's also important to keep in mind that their yields are frequently lower than those of any individual stocks you might choose. That lessens the attraction.

Paying expenses you do not have to pay for is pointless if there isn't a strong case to support them. The ability to obtain a high level of diversity is the true case for mutual funds. The ability to invest in funds that precisely fit your financial goals is another factor working in their favour. But as we're going to discover, by making investments in exchange-traded funds, we can obtain these benefits of mutual funds without any of the drawbacks.

What Is Stock Investing?

Consequently, you now possess a tiny stake in Apple when you purchase shares in the company.

Your entire investment would be $500 if you purchase five Apple shares at a price of $100 each.

Assume for a moment that within the next several weeks, Apple's stock hits $150 a share. Your holdings now have a $750 value, making you $250 richer than you were previously.

It's really cool, huh? That is the fundamental concept of stock investing: Invest when you are aware that the price is low in comparison to the company's intrinsic worth. After that, unwind while the stock price rises steadily, and you profit along the way.

Not every business offers stock for purchase. A business needs to be traded publicly. This indicates that in order for you to buy its stock, the company must be listed on one of the main public stock markets, such as the New York Stock Exchange.

This takes us to the next fundamental of stock investment.

The Stock Market: What Is It?

The market itself has no physical component, despite the existence of real places like the New York Stock Exchange. In the context of trading stocks, "the market" refers to a broad network of financial exchanges and transactions.

Most often, when someone talks about the stock market rising or falling, they're referring to one of the main stock market indices, such as the S&P 500. They are made up of a sizable number of the most significant stocks available throughout the market. The S&P 500, for instance, keeps track of the 500 biggest publicly traded corporations.

When stocks rise, it indicates that there are enough of them growing in value to move the whole market higher. As a result, a rising stock market does not always show a strengthening economy.

The two are related in numerous historical occurrences, but not in 2020 and 2021.

The US economy was in complete collapse due to the coronavirus outbreak. With the exception of a brief but premature meltdown, the stock market rose to all-time highs. As of late 2021, it has continued to grow. The stock market is declining or, at best, staying the same despite improvements in the economy, the addition of jobs, and the distribution of vaccines. These examples demonstrate how the stock market is obviously disconnected from the US economy as a whole.

Chapter 10: How Should We Act During a Crisis?

Individuals who decide to include stocks in their financial portfolio run the risk of two things:

1. Market risk is the standard volatility associated with investments.

2. Human elements, such as emotions and feelings , have nothing to do with investing.

Index-linked ETFs provide passive investment, mitigating the second risk. There is no guarantee that an investment manager can provide, but this kind of investment has shown to be incredibly rewarding over time.

Selecting the investable funds to generate the best long-term returns is all that's left to do. When investing for the first time, you can encounter losses. Even after two or three years of consistent investing, it's feasible that you won't see spectacular returns; more likely, you'll suffer losses. But always remember that index investing is a marathon, not a sprint. Throughout history, a company's worth has fallen and never regained numerous times. But as a long-term investment in a major global stock index, you will never discover an investor who hasn't gained money.

Handling Financial Crisis Situations (or "This Time it's Different!").

We completed a little guided imaging exercise a few pages ago to determine how much we could tolerate in the way of hypothetical and transient financial losses.

Why? Since you would have lost nothing if you had not sold your ETFs. Not even one dime. The quantity of shares that you owned yesterday remains the same. There is just one scenario in which you will experience a loss: selling the securities for less than what you paid for them.

When you are hoping for earnings, seeing red numbers and a minus sign is depressing. Even worse are the statements made by pundits claiming that the current crisis "will forever change the rules of the game." Or they'll say, "We've experienced crises in the past." "But this time it's different."

The James Bond film Tomorrow Never Dies has a line. The antagonist, Elliot

Carver, once said, "There's no news like bad news."

Try searching for financial news from March 2020, December 2019, February 2009, and November 2002 on Google to better understand this. All of these dates have one thing in common: every journalist, fighting for readers, said the end of the world was near.

What do you know? Not at all! It never took place. At the time, a number of events seemed almost apocalyptic, including the Tambora Volcano eruption, World War I, the Spanish flu, World War II, two atomic bombs, the Cold War, the JFK assassination, New Coke, and COVID-19. The market reacts. It falters occasionally, but it always gets back up. Occasionally, like with New Coke, it simply ignores the crisis as if it never happened. Whatever transpires in the global arena, its economy has grown at a rate of almost 10% annually on average.

THE ACTION OF RESERVE

"You should save your money!" is probably something your parents have told you a thousand times over. Here's a breakdown of some of the key arguments supporting your parents' advice if they need clarification on why conserving money is so crucial.

VALUE OF MAKING A SAVING
Having savings gives you more options! Putting money aside is a great habit to get into! Your mother might put some pounds into a different bank account to save for trips. It's as easy as moving funds to a savings account from her primary account. It can mean that you'll be able to take advantage of significant things like a trip to Euro Disney!

Sometimes sacrificing little pleasures can save up money for later, when you're ready to indulge in more decadent treats. Here's another justification for preservation. It implies that in the future, you'll have more money to spend on something more substantial or meaningful to you. It's also definitely not limited to adults!

You'd like to purchase some new headphones, but they're a little pricey. Rather than stopping at the candy store on your way home from school each week, consider putting part of your pocket money into a piggy bank. Before you know it, you'll have enough to purchase the headphones! Another option would be to start a bank savings account.

Money deposited in a bank is kept in a particular account that is registered in your name. When you're ready to spend the money you've saved, you visit the bank and take out a withdrawal. When saving money, it helps to have a goal in mind—a plan for how you want to use the money.

Your outcomes ought to be reliable and long-lasting.

What good is all that self-control and serene concentration if there's nothing to show for it? Since 1956, when he was 25 years old, Warren Buffett has been professionally managing money on his own. He began investing when he was just 11 years old, during the period when Berkshire Hathaway and the Buffett Partnership allow us to most easily track his results. Over an extended period, he has amassed an outstanding record that no one else has been able to match. Buffett amassed an astounding 32% average yearly return before expenses while managing the partnership from 1956 to 1963. That implies that for every $10,000 invested with Buffett at the start of that time, someone with a little bit of foresight and luck would have made an estimated $300,000 when he closed down the partnership.

Over more than 50 years—through recessions and reckless periods of market exuberance, through wars, through nine US Presidents, through disco, punk rock, new wave, hair metal, grunge, boy bands, and all varieties of hip-hop—including bell-bottoms and platforms, the fresh prince, and countless other fads and reality "stars"—that Buffett has proven his success. If you had opted to invest your money in an S&P 500 index fund, you would have received an average return of 9.4%, which is less than half of Buffett's annual return. Compared to the S&P's 25,393.63% gain, Berkshire's book value increased by 2,744,062% total between 1964 and 2020. It is difficult to dispute that Buffett has been anything less than dependable and tenacious over the course of more than 50 years, or that he is capable of something exceptional, considering how extraordinarily skilled at allocating capital.

However, some academics have persisted in their argument and dogmatic teaching that Buffett is an exception and that the market cannot be overcome, beginning in the 1970s and continuing to this day. The "efficient market theory" was the dominant idea at the time and was discussed extensively in business school hallways everywhere. The theory states that the market is fully priced in all available information, without getting too serious about things (though the tweed coat and leather elbow patches can surely be charming). Thus, there is no such thing as a deal or an underpriced or mispriced security because a stock's entire value is always reflected in its price. Therefore, according to proponents of efficient market theory (EMTs), does this imply that Buffett and Graham's years of looking for businesses that were selling at an acceptable margin of safety were in vain?

How absurd it is for them to believe that the market, which is influenced by humans and all of their emotions, as well as some enormous supercomputers that are programmed and managed by humans, could ever be incorrect or overreact. That implies that rather than wasting more time dissecting a corporation, it would be more effective to toss darts at a Wall Street Journal page that is attached to your wall. If there were no inefficiencies in the market, there would be no reason to look for and take advantage of them.

However, that would be false, given that Buffett has consistently generated returns that are above the market. His outcomes demonstrate that he was able to identify undervalued firms, put in place a reasonable system for doing so, and was incredibly successful at it. It gave Buffett immense pleasure to disprove the EMT theorists at that time. In a lecture that became legendary in 1984 at Columbia, the business school where he received his degree, he refuted the arguments of efficient market theory proponents by citing a number of prosperous investors who had established solid track records by applying a firm analysis method developed by Ben Graham and David-Dodd. He named them all "The super investors of Graham-and-Doddsville," of course, and included himself in this number.

The prices on the market are often absurd. Even as the efficient market debate rages on, the expanding area of behavioural finance is steadily weakening the theory's viability by demonstrating that, far from always, market behaviours are the result of rational people acting rationally. It's reasonable to argue that market efficiency has increased since Buffett began. Thanks to a couple of complimentary aspects, it's closer but could be more efficient.

Due to the widespread appeal of renowned investors such as Buffett, an increasing number of investors, both new and experienced, are becoming aware of his strategies and applying them to the markets. Thus, you have all these people searching for comparable stocks and circumstances, making use of a lot of the same easily accessible data. It will take a little more work to get there. Mispriced equities and superior money managers and investors like Buffett will always exist. Fortunately for those who will invest in Graham and Doddsville in the future, Wall Street is packed with smart people who are always coming up with the next big "surefire" strategy to make an investment and persuading the rest of us that "this time is different."

Chapter 4: Products Sold and Purchased in the Market

On the stock market, there are four main categories of goods. These goods are available for purchase and sale. We won't get into short sells or options trading in this part. It will merely look at the product's primary headers with the assumption that you will purchase it since it will become more valuable than alternative options. For novices, options and short sells might be challenging since further discussion of specifics can only be started once you have a thorough grasp of how the market functions.

The items under discussion here are ETFs, mutual funds, stocks, and bonds.

Links

One kind of debt investment is a bond. An investor will give money to a business, bank, or government agency, usually. The investment has a set term and could have a variable or fixed interest rate. Companies, towns, states, and federal governments all use bonds as a means of raising capital for various initiatives. An investor receives bonds instead of a business or other entity going to a bank. A coupon is a piece of paper that represents the bond. The bond can be returned for the payment of accrued interest when the maturity date arrives. Bonds often have a $100 or $1,000 face value. The bond's market price is contingent upon multiple factors, including the creditworthiness of the issuing firm, the duration till maturity, and the bond's coupon rate in relation to the current interest rate.

The purpose of bonds is to provide a long-term, fixed investment. An investor in bonds wants the interest rate to work in their favour. It implies that you will continue to receive 5% interest on a bond you buy with a 5% interest rate even if the interest rate decreases to 4%. But, the bond will only yield 5% interest if the rate rises to 6%, meaning it will lose money.

If bonds pique your attention, you should be aware of the bond's face value at maturity as well as the issue price you will pay for it. When interest is paid on the bond, there are coupon dates. These are usually semi-annual or annual payments. In addition to receiving income, you will also be paid the bond's face value when it matures.

Equities

Individual firm shares are called stocks. From the start of the book, this has been the main topic of discussion. One share can be purchased, giving you a very little ownership stake in the business. It is your privilege to cast votes for board members. It goes without saying that you should purchase enough stock in a company to profit from the selling of those shares. There are two perspectives on stocks.

To take control of the business, you can purchase stock to acquire 50% or more of the company's shares. This is the process by which certain businesses merge with others. It functions only when there is over 50% of the stock available for purchase.

The majority of investors want to purchase a stock at the current price, wait for it to rise in value, and then sell it to profit. By doing this, you are giving up any desire to own stock in the company in favour of only buying and selling on the exchange market for profit. Additionally, since the company is no longer in the IPO stage, it is not profiting from your investment. The fact that dividends are paid out of the company's profits does not change as a result of this. In the event that the business turns a profit, shareholders get a dividend that is determined by their ownership stake in the business as well as the annual profit.

Examine & Assess: Strategies And Tactics

You have probably heard often that research is the key to successful trading. Without question, information is power and plays a crucial role in the decisions you must make. But how precisely do you research a subject for which there is little available? Where and why do you need to search for this information? You will need to take specific actions in order to increase your confidence in your ability to analyse penny stocks and make sure you are obtaining the best profits.

Going to the secretary of state, where the firm is expressly incorporated, is another option you may want to explore. To find out if the corporation is in good standing, you need to get in touch with the Secretary of State. These are all excellent resources to look into for penny stock firms but bear in mind that just because a company appears to have easily accessible information or files reports, it does not necessarily guarantee that investing in it is safe. Examine the words, and exercise caution while choosing an investment. Even if a business is entirely legitimate, it may nevertheless fail, or it may be adept at hiding its real objectives. That element of risk is introduced once more by all of this. This is the reason you will hear this message several times in this book and why it is so crucial to exercise caution.

How To Choose A Penny Stockbroker

Selecting the ideal broker for the task is a helpful recommendation for future success. While the best penny brokers do have fair costs, they also provide a lot of help and are typically much friendlier. Thus, there are undoubtedly many factors to take into account while selecting a penny stockbroker. However, you should conduct the same due diligence on stockbrokers as you would when picking penny stocks to ensure that you are aware of what they have to offer and that you can put enough trust in them.

Take into account if the stockbroker offers a mobile trading platform or an internet one. Find out if the broker's app is available on the internet or even on your phone. This way, no matter where you are, you can determine if a deal is working in your favour or not.

It is also wisest to look into the required minimum payment. Even if many online brokers do not need this, it is best to be certain. Having a fund is certainly important, whether or not there is a deposit fee.

Chapter 2: The Life Beyond

Second Life is an online 3D environment. The Second Life is an online environment that users design, develop, and control. Many individuals who are acquainted with Second Life characterise it as a metaverse. You can be anything you want to be in the virtual world of Second Life. There, you have complete freedom to live your Life as you like and to make it exciting and full of adventures. People who use Second Life on a regular basis, just like you, are the ones who construct the virtual world. Online second lives are ideal if you enjoy interacting with new people you meet online and feel compelled to take things offline. The second Life is open to you if you think it would be interesting to manage a business and even profit from it.

The concept of Second Life wasn't just born on the ground; someone had to come up with it. He created it out of his imagination. Philip Rosedale had always aspired to transcend boundaries and create a potent work of art that would be comparable to everything in the world. He used bytes to make each of these. In November 2002, he started testing it, and six months later, the virtual reality went live for everyone to use.

You can behave as though you were a god in the actual world in Second Life, more like to a mythological deity with the ability to battle, cast spells, and perform other supernatural feats. You will be endowed with the power to perform attacks and have the capacity to teleport and fly to any location in the blink of an eye, regardless of your position in the Second Life. Anytime you choose, you can alter your perspective. The virtual world of Second Life resembles the real world. There are connected areas made up of land, ocean, and sky; you may even erect castles in the air. There are communities and areas, and each of these has its own set of regulations. Depending on the age group, several regions exist. are the owners of the teen grid. Adults cannot access their sector, while users in their age bracket need help accessing the main adult segment. Avatars are used to depict people in the Second Life. There are countless items, structures, sand, and more. And users have made every one of them.

In Second Life, all objects were made with 3D geometric shapes known as prims. About 15,000 prims can be accommodated in each town. These prims are designed in a variety of shapes to facilitate quick transformations into any desired shape. To create the desired profile, apply a few textures to the surface of each prefab. You have the option of creating a transparent body that will blur in the wind or combining shapes to make any form. A dog that moves and barks is an example of a joined or connected profile. The linked prims in the dog were programmed to move in a certain way and make a certain sound.

Purchasing Your First Virtual Property in Chapter 8

Virtual property extends beyond the properties you can purchase that you cannot see; it also includes the ability to convert physical properties into intellectual property. Intellectual properties include things like website addresses, which are nevertheless considered property even though you cannot weigh, taste, or pick them up. Option, derivative, and stock markets are all within the virtual property umbrella. Virtual property includes things like ebooks, movies, music, apps for cell phones, and digital books.

All other properties that are not physical are referred to as intellectual property, such as patents or copyright. Virtual property does exist, but it is not tangible. Virtual characteristics are usually found in virtual worlds, and they cannot live without a virtual world platform. To put it simply, a virtual world is an environment distinct from the real one. This is a non-physical universe. Computers are used to moderate virtual worlds, which are places where people from different backgrounds can live and interact. One profitable strategy to increase your income in the virtual world is to engage in virtual property sales. Selling virtual real estate will be simple, given the growing trend of moving content from the physical world to the digital one.

It is up to computers to control the virtual world. A computer-moderated environment is one in which the computer has complete control over every aspect of it. This implies that if a person owns virtual property, their computer will handle all in-game content associated with the property without requiring them to participate in any activities within the virtual world. You need to understand that your personal computer and the computer that oversees all of these activities are different. The computers are connected and set up in a matrix. There must also be consistency in the virtual world. To be consistent, the virtual world must always be accessible in order to interact with it. The virtual world will appear theoretical, indicating that it does not exist the instant it cannot be reached.

Buying an online property is relatively easy. Check out the map interface for the type of land you are interested in by visiting the virtual property website. Follow the directions to purchase virtual property. Nevertheless, to acquire the ground, you will require cash. On a website called Next Earth, you may purchase virtual real estate. In order to explore the planet using Google Maps,

The Next Earth produced a digital duplicate of the globe.

You can visit the marketplace to look for another item to purchase if the one you want is sold out. Every product that is sold online is represented with a non-fungible token. You can resell them to someone else after you've paid for them and gained access to the property.

Method Seven: Sell Things on Amazon to Make Money

Have you given selling your own products on Amazon any thought as a way to make money? You are able to do so with Amazon. You must select a selling plan in order to begin making money. If you choose the Individual method, you will be paid $0.99 for each item you sell. No matter how many products you sell, the Professional plan costs $39.99 a month. Referral fees are an extra revenue stream for Amazon that varies by product category and is based on a percentage of each sale. To view a pricing summary, visit their pricing page.

One can work as a reseller, as a brand owner, or as both. Resellers find and sell already-available, popular items in Amazon's shops.

Companies who manufacture their own products or purchase products to resell under a private label provide their customers with a customised experience with a wide range of alternatives.

Many vendors handle both jobs. You can select the method that will help you achieve your goals. If you're thinking about creating and selling your products, Amazon can help you with brand design.

I'll presume you're not a parent.

To use Amazon without "the participation of a parent or guardian," an individual needs to be at least eighteen.

According to Amazon's stated terms of service, users under the age of eighteen are not permitted to use the website independently.

You can, therefore, open a selling account under your parents' names in collaboration with them.

Here are the steps to begin selling after that.

• Register for an Amazon account. All you need for this is an active bank account, PAN, and GST number.

• Make a list, save it, and ship it. Finish the product listing and choose from a variety of choices for packaging, delivery, and storage.

• Monitor growth and sales. On desktop and mobile devices, Amazon offers a single dashboard that makes it simple to keep an eye on client requests, sales growth, and payment settlements.

- Receive payment for the sales you make. Once you're a verified Amazon user, payments are automatically transferred to your bank every fourteen days.

Invest some time in becoming acquainted with Amazon's guidelines and policies prior to starting to sell on the website.

Both bull and bear markets

You will frequently hear the terms "bear market" and "bull market" when investing. We want to explain these terms to you. Since investors are the ones who set the direction of the market by their activities, bear and bull markets can also be indicators of their attitudes.

A market that is actively declining is called a bear market. A 20% decline or more usually indicates a bear market.

Investors anticipate that share prices will keep falling as they are currently trending downward. The economy will slow down during this trend, and businesses may begin to lay off workers. Consider a bear. A bear will descend to attack or chase its prey when it is standing erect and using its paws. For this reason, a declining market is represented by a bear.

In contrast, a bull market occurs when the demand is rising. The bull is raising its horns. Prices have been rising steadily during this period, and investors think the trend will continue. In a bull market, employment is high, and the economy is growing.

Generally speaking, long-term activity determines whether a market is bull or bear. Whether positive or negative, short-term swings are more closely associated with a specific occurrence and do not indicate a pattern of any kind. In an attempt to identify direction, markets may also see a string of up-and-down moves. It's not always clear in these situations whether the market is in a bull or bear market.

Both bull and bear markets will significantly impact your assets. You can purchase more securities in a bull market since their value will rise. Investors usually short-sell their holdings during a bad call because they foresee significant losses if they stay in. Some investors will keep clinging to security in the hopes of making money later on. But in a bad market, they will probably lose money before driving it again. Attempting this can be dangerous.

When assessing a market's direction, there are a number of things to take into account. To determine if you are in a bull market or a bear market, you might evaluate these. Always keep in mind that even experienced investors may need help understanding.

¨ There is a high demand but a low supply for securities during a bull market. Few investors are eager to sell, but there are many willing to purchase securities. This shows that people are unwilling to give up their investments, which are increasing in value. Because investors will be vying for available stocks or potentially liquid assets, share prices will climb further. In a bear market, there are more people eager to sell than purchase. Because there is less demand than there is supply, share prices fall dramatically.

The psychology of investors and their perception of the state of the market will also influence whether prices rise or fall. Investors have great expectations during a bull market and are eager to engage in the hopes of generating money. Investors will start transferring money out of active funds and into fixed-income assets during a bear market when sentiment is low. The stock market share price decrease will shake investor confidence, and they will withhold their money until they observe some encouraging movements.

§ The economy and stock market are closely related. Stock prices will decline when businesses are struggling, and consumers are cutting back on their spending. People spend more money when companies are doing well, which raises stock prices.

Think at these several aspects while attempting to identify a bull or bear market. It is safe and dependable to pursue passive investing funds in order to benefit from both market movements. These have a strong long-term success rate and will always offer reduced volatility in erratic markets.

Chapter 1: The Foundations of Cryptocurrency

The word "cryptocurrency" describes a type of virtual money that is exclusively usable online. Real coin or banknote is only possible if you make use of a service that allows you to exchange cryptocurrency for a tangible token. Generally speaking, you can use your computer or phone to trade Bitcoin online without a bank.

To put it more precisely, currencies without a central lender—that is, a nation's central bank—are what constitute cryptocurrencies. They can only be produced in small quantities due to computer encryption before being checked for any additional payment transfers.

Because this process theoretically resembles a gold mine, it is called "mining." Mining becomes more challenging as the algorithm or challenge gets more complex. It takes sophisticated computer processing power to solve these algorithms. Because it costs money to mine them, we are unable to create value out of thin air. Their mathematical laws guarantee that their currencies and their significance are safe from any central bank or government.

And genuine goods. A number of restaurants and clubs have started to use it as payment in recent times. An increasing number of nonprofits are taking.

1.1 How Cryptocurrencies Are Not the Same as Fiat Money

There is mounting evidence that suggests cryptocurrencies may be the form of money in the future, given that some people now utilise electronic money. On the other hand, authorities around the world are vehemently against its entry into the mainstream market.

The public's comprehension of the distinctions between cryptocurrencies and fiat money could be higher.

1.2.2 How Does Fiat Money Operate and What Does It Mean?

The main authorities on this type of money are central banks, which issue and manage fiat currency. These currencies are not backed by any particular item, in contrast to traditional currencies, and can be used as legitimate money. Instead, the credit of the economy is tapped.

In a free market, These currencies will become worthless and lose all of their purchasing value in the event of hyperinflation.

Fiat money was first used in China about the year 1000 AD, and it has since spread over the world. The first commodity to be used as money was gold. President Nixon was only able to stop the US currency's conversion to gold in the 20th century.

1.2.1 Advantages of Fiat Money

Because fiat currencies are so highly stable and controlled, they have remained legal tender in the majority of countries. Compared to alternative forms of money like cryptocurrencies and coins based on commodities, fiat currencies are more stable. This makes it possible for regulators and governments to keep the economy from going into a recession or experiencing inflation.

Fiat money is used to promote trade and store value, but it can only do so because of its stability. It can serve as a numerical account. Central banks have stronger control over many economic variables, including interest rates, lending availability, and liquidity, in order to maintain a robust and stable economy.

1.2.22 Cons of fiat money

Fiat money is thought to be a stable currency, although this is only sometimes the case. Over time, economic downturns have exposed some of the shortcomings of fiat money. Because gold is infinitely produced and therefore immune to inflation or recession, many people believe that it is a more stable kind of money. Because of the persistent rise in prices throughout the world and the notion that central banks control the economy, cryptocurrencies are necessary.

Purchasing a company's shares indicates that you are investing in the company, which is the essence of value investing. The value investor buys the shares at a price that is either less than or equal to the asset's value because he is concerned with both the asset's intrinsic value and potential future earnings. All of these are the fundamental ideas of value investing. The ability to evaluate or compare the worth of a corporation to potential future estimates is at issue.

Your worry as a value investor is different from the markets. To determine whether to purchase or sell stocks, you don't turn to the marketplace. In addition to what the chart for a ticker symbol tells you, you consider other elements.

Buy an Enterprise

Buying stocks requires you to think of the transaction as acquiring a business. Yes, you are purchasing a chunk of it, but only some of it. Even in the event that you only buy one share. You must acquire this mindset for one simple reason: it compels you to dedicate yourself to the business, which is the one thing you must do to succeed. You're making this commitment because your investment will yield a healthy return.

The majority of investors who participated in the dot com boom and bust may believe that they closely monitored the companies they worked with. After getting news information, they either watched or read it. In actuality, though, the majority of them should have looked more closely at the company's foundation. They should have cared to investigate the underlying principles of the businesses they were investing in. They didn't give their tactics any thought, and they didn't even check to see if each company had any competitive advantage. What those investors did and what ethical value investors do differ primarily in that the first group fell for the hype, while the latter group constantly looked to see if the stock price was a good deal or overpriced and about to crash. Value investment is distinct from other types of investing in this way.

Proper Evaluation

Investors in value make sure to evaluate the company first. That's the same as what you do when you're going to purchase real estate. Before you spend any money, you need to have it valued. However, value investing entails far more in the appraisal process than it does with real estate. You need to review all available data and statistics. Not only should you consider what the charts indicate, but you also need to look at the numbers. Examining the value and how it relates to the present market price is the main goal here. How come? to determine whether investing in a business is warranted for you or not?

Value investing goes beyond simple Wall Street-style investment analysis. It involves examining the core metrics that determine how well a firm performs. Metrics, including capital structure, profitability, and productivity, are under discussion. In order to determine if there is still potential for growth or whether there will likely be a significant decline in the not-too-distant future, you then take it a step further and look at how these measures correspond with the most recent news about the company.

Innovative Finance Solutions

Other than traditional home loans, there are different ways to use capital. One of the key differences between successful real estate developers and other investors is their ability to identify creative ways to use means for land contributions. Many people don't start with large amounts of money to contribute, and it's possible that they need to fulfil all the requirements for credit or a home loan. What are those people doing? Yes, that is where the "inventive" aspect is needed. You should be well on your road to success if you can figure out how to approach shrewdly back deals.

Here is an example of something I did when I first started investing in houses. I needed money when the whole Nicaragua thing went south. However, there were certain offers that I was genuinely interested in. I could have contributed roughly $10,000 at that point. This was around 2011, when the recession was still fully underway, so I could easily use $10,000 and a house loan to buy a fantastic investment property. I knew I could accomplish this for one property, but how would I buy additional once that $10,000 was gone?

Good day, creative finance!

At this point, I obtained a venture partner for multiple properties.[5] As an

An accomplice in speculating had various arrangements totalling $10,000 available. But how might I give him something in return for utilizing his funds? We decided to purchase the deals with my credit and his cash. I took out home loans in my name, completed nearly everything, and he paid the upfront installments. He offered the money, and I assumed the risk. We both agreed that this created a 50/50 commitment split. Upon buying the properties, we decided to divide all the benefits and losses equally 50/50. Whenever we collected money, it was always him for half and me for the other half. In the event that substantial expenses arose, we divided them evenly. Should we decide to sell, we would divide the gains or losses equally. From his perspective, the arrangement was excellent since it allowed him to save money without any restrictions or hitch (yes, you can apply for a restricted amount of home loans in your name). Furthermore, because I invested no money in the properties, I ended up with essentially infinite returns.

That's only one option among many for creative solutions to funding. Credits from sources other than traditional home loans could be included in alternative financing options. It's possible that you fold value into another property from one. The possibilities for financing conjectures are endless. The important thing is to make sure you understand the details of each option and select one that looks appropriate for your circumstances.

Developing creative finance solutions is the key to creating a kingdom. People who have already completed the task without assistance can provide you with some helpful advice, but they can only assist you up to this stage. Organizing creative financing agreements is like going through a transitory phase for successful financial supporters; very few domain owners achieve success without creative financing.

The Essentials Of Investing In The Stock Market

It would be best if you comprehended the fundamentals of the stock market in order to succeed in it. In general, the stock market operates just like any other market. A price is agreed upon by buyers and sellers getting together. Price is, therefore, the most important tool available to investors for making trades. So, let's talk about how equities are priced on the market.

How to Set Stock Prices
The fundamental component of stock pricing is supply and demand. To put it simply, prices rise when there is a high demand (many buyers) and a low supply (few suppliers). On the other hand, prices decrease when there is a big supply (many sellers) and low demand (few sellers). Perfect market pricing exists when buyers and sellers are on an equal footing. In a free market, this is the general rule that applies to all

commodities. The majority of price activity is determined by supply and demand, unless a market is manipulated.

But price in financial markets is also determined by other factors. Psychological factors are primary. What we mean by "psychological" is what potential investors think will or won't occur. For example, investors would swarm to acquire a company if they believe it is undervalued. As a result, the price will increase due to their desire to purchase stock in this company. In the same vein, a company's stock price will drop if investors believe there is a problem with it.

Additionally, investors may hesitate to buy or sell due to the state of the economy. For instance, investors might be much more cautious during a recession. After all, they might be worried about how the present state of the economy would affect them in the long run.

Furthermore, a company's stock valuation is heavily influenced by its management, competition, and financials. A company is a winner if it leads its industry, has strong financials, and recognized leadership. Don't be shocked, though, if an investor places a long-shot wager. These are unproven businesses that may be ready for a resurgence following a difficult period. But if you wager on long shots, use caution. There always needs to be assurance that things will come to pass.

Considering the Future

You must gaze into the past in order to glimpse into the future. You may predict the future with stock prices by examining the past price movement. Every company has historical information about how its market valuation has behaved. With this knowledge, you may focus on the future. You can predict possible outcomes based on its historical trend. Naturally, nothing can be guaranteed. Even so, you can obtain a clear image of what is ahead.

As such, you need to learn how to read charts and graphs. These components comprise the graphical depiction of the price action data. A line graph is the most typical type of graph. When displaying the trend behaviour of a stock, line graphs work flawlessly. Additionally, you will be able to predict future events based on their patterns.

We refer to the examination of numerical data as "technical analysis." Technical analysis is essential to decision-making. You are speculating if you base your investing selections on your personal opinion of value. As a result, in order to establish your assumptions about a stock reasonably, you need objective data. If not, there is an exponential increase in the danger of losing on a deal.

How to Select Successful Stocks

Putting together a portfolio is the most crucial aspect of investing. This is your holding for potential gains in the future,therefore, it makes sense to conduct a thorough study. The majority of investors buy stocks quickly and with very little investigation. Considering that you want to store these equities for a number of years, this doesn't make much sense. So why choose to buy a company for numerous years after only ten minutes of research? Selecting profitable stocks requires more attention, but it can be done quickly with study.

First criterion: Is the industry expanding?

Is the stock in an industry that is anticipated to grow over the next few years at a high, nearly exponential rate? If so, search for stores in this category to identify the market leaders, major rivals, and emerging small businesses whose earnings are increasing more quickly than average. One useful method for identifying emerging sectors is to pose the question, "What will be more relevant in the future?"

Your mind should be filled with numerous ideas. Put them in writing and explain how they can make an existing approach better or solve an issue. Now look at stocks in that industry; five to ten should do the trick. Put them in writing and ensure that you are aware of the following:

• P/E Ratio; • Growth Rate; • Market Capitalization; • Earnings Per Share; • Dividend Yield; • Total Addressable Market

This is significant since it illustrates the extent of the company's growth potential. With Apple's market capitalization at 2.33 trillion, a 2.33 trillion increase in market capitalization is required for the stock to double. Apple will make a wonderful value stock because it's a terrific firm that consistently meets expectations with expansion; however, if you're looking for a growth stock, it wouldn't be a smart pick because it has matured to the point where it can't develop exponentially.

A useful metric for assessing a stock is the price-to-earnings ratio or P/E ratio. However, this is entirely stock-specific, as certain companies have a premium P/E ratio due to projected growth. For instance, the P/E ratio of Tesla is at 424.12, despite the stock rising 2000% over the last five years. This is a crucial criterion for value investors, but since most growth companies don't turn a profit, growth investors should focus on it only a little.

Growth Rate: You must consider the growth rate when searching for growth stocks. The business should be expanding by double digits, ideally by more than 30%. The company will probably not turn a profit at these rates, but that's okay because we think it will turn a profit and become a leader in its industry eventually. Shopify is a perfect example of growth. Their yearly revenue growth is as follows:

Revenue for 2018 was $1.073 billion, up 59.4% from the previous year.

Revenue for 2019 was $1.578 billion, up 47.05% from the previous year.

Revenue in 2020: $2.929 billion, up 85.63% from 2019.

Shopify's sales increased by 82.25% year over year to $3.853 billion for the twelve months that ended on June 30, 2021.

Considering that it was profitable and able to grow at an 86% rate, these results are amazing. It would be best if you held these stocks because they will increase in value. In just six years, the price of Shopify has increased from $28 at IPO to $1,424.5 today—a 5,008% gain! When it comes to stocks, growth rate matters a lot.

1.4 The Blockchain Technology's Foundations

Although we could write a book on blockchain technology alone, if you want to trade Bitcoin or any other cryptocurrency, you must grasp the fundamentals.

Since blockchain is a decentralized ledger, anyone can access and verify its contents. This is essential for any non-physical good since, in contrast to material goods like socks or sweets, we need proof of a transaction in case something goes wrong. Proof that Steve paid for the socks John sold him would serve as an example of this requirement for documentation. The only information on the blockchain will be the transactions that took place between Steve and John's accounts.

Before, in order to verify that the transaction had actually happened, we had to depend on a third party, like a bank. The bank would then take its cut of the total transaction after that. Since the bank's information is private, we would have to have faith in them to carry out their duties. Thanks to blockchain technology, we have an entirely accurate record of the activity that is occurring, and everybody can see it. Additionally, you won't have to pay a middleman any more money. The only fee is what it costs to keep the blockchain up to date.

If blockchain is only used for financial purposes, countries without a stable banking system will greatly benefit from it. Every transaction has a time and date stamp included and is recorded as a block. These blocks can only be altered with being visible to everyone. This resolves the "double-spending dilemma," which arises when digital assets, like cryptocurrencies, have the capacity to be spent multiple times. We can tell, thanks to the blockchain, that Steve has already paid John with his money, which stops him from trying to pay Sally with the same funds. The blockchain fosters mutual trust across all participants, which is essential when conducting financial transactions.

We might also utilize the platform to store other kinds of data that need to be transparently accessible to the general public. This can range from vote records in elections to a self-executing contract between two parties that takes effect after both parties have fulfilled their obligations. Because blockchain acts as both an auditor and an independent in some circumstances, it eliminates the need for a middleman or independent auditor. Technology may replace lawyers, accountants, and a significant chunk of the financial services industry. Many of the non-financial applications of blockchains are still purely speculative, though, lest we get ahead of ourselves.

The foundation of the American way of life has been an obligation, particularly in the last ten years. This would never have happened if the dollar hadn't been the world's money saver.

A nation, a company, or a daily existence cannot sustain itself indefinitely on debt. The instalment is due eventually.

The Covid outbreak set off an event (downturn) that was long overdue.

If you are aware of your opponent and yourself, you shouldn't be afraid of what will happen after 100 fights. If you are aware of yourself but not the enemy, you will suffer a loss for every victory you achieve. In the unlikely event that you are unaware of your own identity or that of your opponent, you will give up every fight.

Ah, Sun Tzu, The Warfare Craft

Nothing can stop change. There are two possible responses to it:

- Accepting it.
- Modifying your speculative strategy accordingly.
- Reaping the benefits of the opportunities that present themselves.

Alternatively, you could be afraid of it, refuse to change, turn down opportunities that present themselves, see your benefits diminish, and even lose wealth and money.

Market Cycles: Acclimate Yourself

Market cycles have always been significant. Thirty-three of these cycles have occurred since about 1854, with an average interval between peaks of a little over 56 months. Beginning about 1960, four cycles have lasted nine years or more. The most recent financial development took 126 months to materialize before the Covid appeared out of nowhere.

Markets consist of billions of exchanges, and the housing market is no exception. The overall economy is one of those business sectors. Over the years and decades, the economy has swung up and down.

And what impact do these cycles have on our delayed plenty and Freedom setting? Opportunity doesn't always imply retirement; it can indicate choices and decisions. Most find them to be deeply upsetting, ruining goals and dreams from the past. A fresh start, a redo.

When one eventually runs out of time, they are left with what Henry David Thoreau described as "men carrying on with lives of calm desperation." "Carrying on with lives of regret" is what I would term it.

What is Investing? in Chapter 1.

It's vital to take some time to define investing before delving into the several avenues for generating income. As you can see, only a few people truly understand what investing entails. They mistakenly believe that all schemes to make money are investments, even if this isn't the case.

Many have long debated the definition of investing and what constitutes an investment. Benjamin Graham, the father of value investing, was the first to define the term accurately. In the early to mid-1900s, Graham managed money well and led a successful life.

Whether it was one of the two World Wars or the Great Depression, he lived through a time of economic turmoil that nearly destroyed him. Graham became exceedingly conservative as a result, focusing first on defining what investment actually is.

As per Graham's definition, investment is an intellectual endeavour with little chance of failure. That definition offers us nothing as regular investors. Ultimately, what exactly is intelligence, and how is it possible to determine the likelihood of failure? Saying that an investor should always strive to aim for maximum gain while incurring as little risk as feasible could be the best way to redefine this concept.

In this world, there is no such thing as zero risk. You need to be willing to take chances and possibly lose some money in order to make money. There is no profit if there is no risk. However, as not all opportunities are created equal, this does not suggest that you should always take large risks.

Some people may find the risk an opportunity presents to be too great, while others may be able to tolerate that degree of risk. The key to effective investing is ultimately determining the level of risk you are ready to accept and matching it to the desired return.

As you may expect, this is a matter of personal experience, which is why "missing out" does not exist. The only investments you lose out on are those that you ought to have been aware of but decided against. Therefore, it wouldn't be a loss to lose out on Amazon's expansion if your area of expertise is investing in insurance firms. There is nothing you can overlook that you are unaware of.

Looking at major media channels and social media feeds, this way of thinking is not particularly common. These publications promote everything as a wise investment, including technology and oil and gas firms. People are pushed narratives by them.

How many times have you heard that investment will fundamentally change as a result of COVID? Or that things will alter due to 5G? or that everything will change as China grows? Since change is a constant, why should any oneoccurrence be so exceptional that it alters "everything"? These media sources thrive on promoting stories that, in turn, purport to be able to assist you in understanding. It's similar to them inventing a problem and then asserting that they can fix it.

Preventing the issue from the start is preferable.

Rule 3: ASSEMBLISH WITH A SAFETY MARGIN

Almost many seasoned investors started their careers by reading Benjamin Graham's The Intelligent Investor. It is, by far, the best book on investing ever written, according to Warren Buffett. What makes it so unique? One of the reasons is that it introduced the crucial concept of the "Margin of Safety."

When an investment is purchased at a lower value than its worth, a margin of safety is established based on conservative assumptions. The concept of a margin of safety is that you want to purchase a business at a low enough price that your acquisition may be entirely successful and you would retain little.

Rule 4: Take responsibility for your homework and knowledge.
There needs to be a replacement for doing your own work. Purchasing a stock because it looks attractive, your uncle suggested it, or CNBC recommended it is a surefire way to lose money.
Wealthy investors are aware of their assets. They purchase stocks of companies whose products they believe in. Successful investors go above and beyond to examine the company's finances to ensure they are getting everything. However, you will be persuaded to invest in it once you have a thorough understanding of the company.
"You must understand what you own and why you own it." -Thomas Lynch

Rule 5: Remain calm and reasonable; don't go with the crowd.

Regretfully, I am obligated to say that this recipe will not work. The most skilled investigators are those who can combat this urgency, restore composure with a tree, and restore integrity with a bubble.

The wisest investor in history, Warren Buffett, once said, "Be greedy when others are greedy, and greedy when others are greedy!"

Rule 6 states that you shouldn't have too many baskets, but you also shouldn't put all of your eggs in one.

One of the most important strategies for your portfolio is diversification so that if one stock fails, it won't sink the entire ship. We will make a mistake even though we don't think we will. Because even the masters do, we are unable to put all of our eggs in one basket. There is power in diversity.

However, studies indicate that in most markets, The more you differentiate yourself from that, the less you know about each investment (see Rule #4). While diverging is important, prioritize your finest ideas because they are always better than your 100th best idea!

1.3. Turning Around the Financial Exclusion Trend

There is another story that is unfolding behind the scenes of this amazing one. After 25 years of the internet, sending money from here to a non-European country through a bank actually takes three to five days. Sending cash will always cost you between $30 and $40, assuming the country you are sending it to is not a defenceless one. If so, that trade will unquestionably be more expensive and take much longer. A massive conglomerate of closed, corrupt systems that are snatching money from the world's most wretched people. There are between three and a half and four billion people on the internet today, yet slightly over one billion of them have banking and full access to financial services. Imagine what would happen if you released banking as an app to every person with a $20 Android smartphone.

More quickly than cell phone usage, this will transform the planet. Imagine a $20 Android phone that is shipped to a Kenyan hamlet. However, it's now a bank rather than just a communication tool. Not a bookkeeping system, but a bank. It can send and receive assets from anywhere in the world. It can lend money or obtain advances for a house loan, buy seeds for a farm, or provide disaster relief. It can directly connect to billions of people worldwide, completely eschewing traditional banking. We have the next ten years to complete this.

When you give everyone in this society the ability to receive extensive financial consideration, the world will drastically shift. It may occur to you that banks must take this action. You would be mistaken. Serving people in mistreated countries with terrible state-run governments who have little money, little availability, and little access to identification is not genuinely productive. Similarly, banks are essentially criminal organizations and hoodlums in the majority of those countries. Or, on the other hand, it is extremely ambiguous from the local crowd.

CHAPTER 8: The Process of Setting Prices

S

As an investor, you must have a thorough awareness of the various elements that affect an option's value before you go into the realm of options trading. The components consist of the stock's intrinsic value, current price, expiration date, interest rate, volatility, and paid cash dividends. It is possible to come across many options pricing models that utilize every one of these elements to calculate the market's option fair value. Options trading is similar to other investment types in a few aspects; all you have to do is comprehend the various components that go into their price.

Let's start by discussing the four main factors that influence the price of an option: volatility, intrinsic value, current stock price, and expiration date. The stock price as of right now is rather clear. The option price is directly impacted by changes in the stock price, although not in the same way. A call option's price is likely to increase in tandem with a stock's price increase, whereas the put option's price is likely to decrease. The put and call prices move in the opposite direction when the stock price starts to decline.

inherent worth

It is the amount that any given option would be worth if it were exercised right now. To put it simply, intrinsic value is the total amount that the strike price of an option is within the money. Additionally, it refers to the part of an option's price that remains intact while the expiration date appears to be approaching or having passed. Any call or put option's intrinsic value can be easily calculated using the following method:

The intrinsic value of a call option is equal to USC – CS, where USC denotes the current price of the underlying stock, and CS is the call strike price.

The effective nature of the potential financial benefit that could arise from exercising the concerned option right away can be directly reflected in the intrinsic option value. It can also be thought of as an option's minimal value. Options that trade at the money or out of the capital have no intrinsic value.

The put option's intrinsic value is equal to PS - USC, where PS is the set strike price, and USC is the current price of the underlying stock.

Let's take an example where Elegant Electric (EE) stock is selling out at $35. Since the option holder can execute the option to purchase shares of EE at $20, turn around, and then automatically sell them out in the market for $35 and make a profit of $15, the EE 20 call option would have an intrinsic value of $15 ($35-$20 = $15).

In order for your house to sell, whether you like it or not, you will almost always need to put some work into marketing it. What is marketing, exactly? Creating a plan to promote a thing is called marketing. Sales, advertising, promotion, and research are all included in marketing.

Examine your neighbourhood's market and the going rates for similar items. You'll need to be abreast of market developments during the entire sales process, which might take months. This is important since you can be in talks for a while, and knowing how your property is currently doing will help you make wise judgments during the negotiation.

To draw in a large number of potential buyers, advertising is necessary. If multiple people are interested in buying your house, you could start a bidding war, which would increase the sale price. How ought one to market oneself? Utilize every tool at your disposal for advertising, including the internet, targeted mailings, newspapers, flyers, word-of-mouth, and special trade pamphlets.

You can post pictures of your house on a number of real estate investing websites. A comprehensive marketing strategy includes these online marketing resources. Select a popular website and provide attractive pictures of the exterior and interior of your property. Consider adding a virtual tour.

If Sales Aren't High Enough
The real estate market experiences fluctuations. Selling your investment property could be easy or difficult, depending on where you are in the cycle. You could have to wait for purchasers if the market has tanked or reached a standstill. This may irritate you because it can tie up money and make you wait for a profit.

There are several strategies you could employ to escape this predicament.

1. If you can afford it and it's your primary residence, wait it out. Every one to five years, the market typically swings, and you could profit by selling during the next upswing.

2. Examine your property from the buyer's point of view and make any necessary adjustments. Your home will appreciate in value and attract more buyers as a result of this. Take into mind any factors that can act as a deterrent. To lessen the impact of a noisy roadway, for instance, shut the windows and turn on some relaxing music.

3. Make the house visible. Arrange some flower arrangements, dim the lights, play some relaxing music, bake some freshly made cookies to create a cosy aroma, and get ready to serve some refreshments to your guests. Put a flyer with lots of eye-catching pictures, a summary of the property's advantages, and your contact details on the property. Allow the customer to visualize themselves residing there.

Buyers want a home in which they feel pride.

4. Convince your neighbors to help you enhance the community's aesthetics.
5. Verify again that the house's pricing is correct. Due to the frequent fluctuations in markets, your pricing could not be competitive in the current market.

Take into consideration taking the property off the market for a while before re-listing it after double-checking your pricing if you've tried these tips and it still has yet to sell. Long-term property listings lead prospective purchasers to assume that there is a problem with the property. Promote your house widely. Putting forth more effort to sell your home can only increase your profit margin.

Observe the Physical Laws

As you are well familiar, "What goes around comes about." In the East, it is referred to as "Karma". It is actually the law of physics known as "cause-effect," or Newton's Third Law of Motion, which states that "for every action there is an equal or opposite reaction." Any pond can have its tranquillity upset by a single pebble thrown into it. The ripples were the result, and you were the reason. Till harmony can be restored, the waves expand and then return. Discordant actions have the same effect. Until balance is restored, they leave the world and return to that person. It's critical to let go and live. If you consider matter to be the only thing that exists, you may conclude that you are free to do as you choose, injure anyone you select, and escape punishment. Things operate differently. You will eventually receive what you put in, even though it might work for a long.

There are rules in metaphysics, just as there are in physics. All peoples and all nations must adhere to them. Consider Germany and Japan in World War II as an example. Both countries first achieved notable triumphs. Every country benefited from the perception that they were unstoppable. The horrors they had perpetrated had crushed them. Because of the way China's government handled the COVID-19 outbreak and attempted to conceal it, the country will likely endure something akin to what happened in Vietnam, albeit less catastrophic. One, given that we and other leaders are aware of how precarious it was for us to outsource vital supplies to China, China is likely to lose a lot of manufacturing contracts.

Let's explore the concept of Karma in more detail. Giving more than you receive will result in receiving more. This implies that you will receive back what you offer to the world. Put another way, people will give back to you more the more you help them. Doing something is vital because it is a part of who you are, not because it will benefit you personally. That is correct. It is not a theoretical notion of a do-gooder. If you are driven to serve others without looking for or anticipating anything in return, this will work in your day-to-day activities. This is not a noble idea. Be your most selfless, joyful self!

You might believe that I'm naturally kind, but you're not. My recommendation? Modify your character. Nothing is expected of you in return. Rather, love doing good things that benefit others. Eventually, helping others will become second nature to you since it will bring you happiness. Acquire knowledge about oneself. We have the freedom to select who we want to be because we are human. Take pride in the things that fill you with pride.

Let's say you are a business owner and an attack targets you. How should you proceed? Assume you are a business owner, and a competitor or vendor files a lawsuit against you because of a perceived or actual grievance. Collect all the information before responding and intensifying the situation. Assemble all employees within your organization with knowledge of the vendor or potential causes of the conflict. This group should ascertain the truth about what transpired and talk about any concerns or difficulties that may come up.

The following should be provided in response to these queries: "What can I do to get them what or want?" To get the lawsuit dropped, you may offer them a contract or an advantage in a different part of the business or nation. Instead of inciting or exacerbating disorder, you seek to restore balance to the situation. Sometimes, one of the best ways to accomplish this is to discover a win-win solution. It could be beneficial for your group to discuss ideas and evaluate how various activities affect those who are following your example. What specifically are you hoping to get out of the leader of the other side?

You have two options: engage in combat that might damage your company or extend a peace offer that might assist in resolving the issue. If you treat people with respect and compassion, most cases will be settled. If you want to be a friend, you have to be one.

In this world, some are uncontrollably crazy. It is inappropriate to oppose bullies. Occasionally, people will file lawsuits for no apparent reason other than to obtain something for nothing. These individuals frequently only comprehend one thing, which is, to put it simply, a punch to the nose. If so, proceed as necessary, but only after attempting to reason with them. It is not appropriate for you to take a literal punch to the nose. If you can create and sustain harmony among others, you have a higher chance of things working out in your favour. The advantages don't end when everything fits together.

Determine And Make Investments

Based On The Type Of Market

Investing in the stock market is always a good idea. There are always possibilities to generate money, regardless of market sentiment; however, the tactics you employ will undoubtedly vary based on the nature of the market. Making sure you are accurately interpreting the market is the first step towards ensuring you are utilizing your capital to its fullest potential. The first stage in choosing the correct stocks and mutual funds to invest in is figuring out the market type. However, this kind of investing is for the bold. A 529 savings plan is an excellent option due to its low risk and low maintenance requirements. It takes more than just intelligence to succeed in the stock market; you also need to put in a lot of effort, perseverance, and time.

Markets are cyclical, so most investors will see extended periods when the market performs as bullish or bearish.

Rapid changes do occur, but slower declines or increases in market activity are much more typical. It is imperative to look for a trend or pattern that indicates the decline in performing markets in order to allocate your resources where they would be most effective. While there are no magic bullets for staying ahead of market developments, there are tools developed over decades that can benefit all kinds of investors.

An excellent indicator of a market's health is the advance/decline line. The best way to conceptualize this line is as the slope of the closing up-to-down stock ratio. The advance/decline line would be determined by first determining the number of stocks that finished ahead of yesterday's closing price and then the number that ended below the previous day's closing price. For instance, if there were only five stocks traded on the New York Stock Exchange. Assume that three equities finished higher and two stocks ended lower. Then, we compute our advance/decline line by dividing the final values of our three positive stocks by the absolute values of our two negative stores. That puts our advance/decline line at 1.5. This data point only applies to today; subsequent days will yield new data points. This line's slope is a good indicator of a weak stock market if it begins to turn below 1. An indicator of positive growth is when the slope is greater than 1. Finding these patterns is very useful, as it will be far more accurate in predicting a market decline than the Dow Jones Industrial Average and comparable averages from other exchanges.

When determining whether a market is bullish or bearish, investors are typically informed by the market's average. An average with a percentage change is included each time the market data is prepared to measure the performance of the Dow Jones Industrial Average. This figure is not the same as the advance/decline ratio. Most market averages are a group of stocks that were set decades ago and do not convey the same type of useful information that they once did. Averages were put together for the same goal of the advance/decline line but functioned a little differently. A market average is a basket of stocks that are traded on a market. These stocks were picked because the firms behind them are such huge financial powers that it was assumed the health of these few companies would reveal the overall health of the entire market. It was a simple solution, a solution that require a lot of data and one that provide a great way to spread the strength of the company's powerful enough to be listed on the average. Once companies are added to a market average, they are almost never taken out. It is simply through tradition that these numbers still share any importance and are still read on every radio and television show describing markets. Still, the numbers themselves should not be used to judge market health. Once you have instead used the advance/decline ratio to determine the type of market that you are in, you can then move on to forming the best strategy.

How MuchAreNftsWorth?

In theory, anybody can tokenize theirwork to sellas an NFT, but interest has been fuelled by recent headlines of multi-million-dollar sales.

On 19 February, an animated Gif of Nyan Cat - a 2011 memeofaflyingpop-tartcat - sold for more than $500,000 (£365,000).

A few weeks later, musicianGrimessold some of herdigitalart for more than $6m.

It is notjustart that istokenised and sold. Twitter's founder JackDorsey has promoted an NFT of the first-ever tweet, withbidshitting $2.5m.

Christie'ssale of an NFT by digital artistBeeplefor $69m (£50m) setanewrecord for digitalart.

FrenchfirmSorare, whichsells football trading cardsin the formofNFTs, has raised $680m (£498m).

But as withcrypto-currencies, thereare concerns about the environmentalimpactof maintaining theblockchain.

'Side-eyeing Chloe' Clem tosell iconic memeas NFT

What's stoppingpeoplecopying the digital art?

Nothing. Millions of people have seen Beeple'sartthatsoldfor $69m and the image hasbeencopiedand shared countless times.

In many cases, the artist evenretains the copyrightownershipoftheir work, so they cancontinueto produce andsellcopies.

But the buyer of the NFT owns a "token" that proves theyownthe "original" work.

Somepeoplecompareit to buyingan autographed print.

Is this a bubble?

A day before his record-breakingauction, Beeple -
whoserealnameisMikeWinkelmann -

toldthe BBC: "I actually do thinktherewill be a bubble, to be quite honest. "And I think wecouldbeinthatbubblerightnow." Many are even more sceptical.

DavidGerard, authorofAttackofthe 50-foot Blockchain, saidhe saw NFTsasbuying "official collectables", similar to trading cards.

"Therearesomeartists absolutely making bankonthisstuff... it'sjustthat you probably won't," he warned.

Thepeopleactuallyselling the NFTs are "crypto-grifters", he said.

"The sameguyswho'vealwaysbeen at it, trying to come upwithanew form ofworthless magic bean that they can sellformoney."

FormerChristie'sauctioneerCharlesAllso pp said the concept ofbuyingNFTs made "nosense".

"Theideaofbuying something whichisn'tthereisjust strange," he told the BBC.

"I think peoplewho invest in it are slightmugs, but I hope they don't lose their money."

What happens if my online broker goes bust?

Another broker may step in and buy the business. Then, your account will be safe and be registered with the new purchaser. Otherwise, if the broker is regulated, a sovereign government may step in. In this case, depending on the regulating country, some or all of your funds and assets will remain safe.

5 top online brokers for beginners

You are going to have to do your own research to track down the perfect broker for you. A lot depends on what assets you want to trade in. But what it all boils down to is which country you live in. You can ask around on the internet to find brokers which serve your particular country of residence.

And do not be discouraged. The online brokerage market is fast-growing. Brokers are bringing out new services and extending their scope all the time.

Below are 5 brokers to review as a starting point.

We have no affiliation with any of the brokers mentioned. So it is from a completely independent perspective that we recommend eToro as your first port of call. With 20m customers in 100 countries, eToro has invested heavily in making its online brokerage easy to use with plenty of learning materials and investment options that develop all the time.

If you are a US citizen, then TD Ameritrade offers a good experience for beginners. In the US, other excellent broker sites are provided by Charles Schwab, Vanguard and Fidelity.

For European traders, the market could be better developed in the UK and US. Consider eToro, but also look at Degiro, which offers good access to European citizens and is developing a good name for itself.

We are constantly searching for materials that will demonstrate real-world procedures. We will examine the beginnings of three distinct real estate investors in this chapter.

House Exchange:

We talked about how this was the most straightforward real estate investment. Here's one Florida success story from Tom.

This narrative illustrates the idea that you can never be sure where to look for a buyer or sale. A little over three months ago, Tom was having lunch in a café as he got ready to give a lecture about wholesaling. Suddenly, out of nowhere, a man approached him and asked to see Tom's clothing. They swapped business cards at this point and got to speak about how the man was a realtor before moving on.

Tom got a call from the relator a few months later, telling him that he was selling his house. He was facing foreclosure on his own, having inherited the house from his mother.

For the property, the realtor was requesting a price between $165,000 and $168,000. On a ski lake, the house has three bedrooms and two and a half bathrooms. Tom offered the realtor $162,000, and she graciously accepted.

Tom talked to another person who showed interest in buying the house, even though he still needed to sign the deal. Tom informed him the price and the man said he was looking for a house like this one, so he would look at it and probably buy it.

About twenty days after the deal with the seller was signed and concluded, Tom's friend signed a new contract.

It took Tom twenty days to consummate that purchase.

Tom managed to make a little money in a matter of hours of work.
He just told people what he did for a living.

Could You Invest?
Now that you understand "what is speculation definition" and how it might help you create abundance, the next step is to consider how you can help. Before deciding to make a contribution, keep in mind these two very important points.

1. Identify Your Needs in Terms of Money

Analyze your financial situation as it relates to risk tolerance, investment goals, and other factors such as the size of your family, the number of people you are acquiring, and your life goals. You may even seek assistance from a financial advisor. It will help you identify the right decisions and provide answers to any queries regarding "how venture affects you."

2. Diversification of Ventures

Create a diversified financial portfolio in line with your project goals by allocating your resources across a range of instruments to maintain the ideal balance between risks and rewards.
Similarly, when contemplating "what does speculation mean" and "where can I contribute?" think about prioritizing the tools that provide your loved ones with protection. It may include additional security measures such as term plans and other similar instruments (ULIP complete structure: Unit Linked Insurance Plan). Consider the goals of the project in order to generate appropriate returns.

3. Duration

You should also be aware that, regardless of the duration, it is difficult to say how someone is affected by conjecture. This is the reason you should consider how much time you have before turning your passions into a profitable venture. This is a crucial factor in determining your speculative objectives. You can choose between short-term and long-term reserves based on your needs.

4. Regular Evaluation

Because market forces affect reserves, it is essential that you periodically carefully review them. If the returns on your portfolio aren't very high, consider correcting them.

You can peruse a variety of growth methods offered by Max Life, such as the Guaranteed Income Plan, the Smart Wealth Plan, and the Savings Advantage Plan, and that's only the tip of the iceberg, depending on your venture and reserve money destinations.

Guidelines for Buying Cryptocurrency
It's wise to go by certain rules while investing in cryptocurrencies in order to maximize your profits and protect you from potential fraud. Here are the top five guidelines for trading cryptocurrencies.

Devoting time to researching cryptocurrencies
We have said this time and time again. Invest in instruments that you are familiar with. It's advisable to wait to enter the market until you feel ready if you don't know how to profit from investing in cryptocurrencies.

This claim is supported by the idea that there is a greater chance of error while investing if you need more understanding of the subject matter. Think about this scenario:

You are fully aware that the term "digital money" refers to cryptocurrencies. You need to understand the many types of cryptocurrencies and their values completely. Thus, you could be sold a cryptocurrency exchange-traded fund (ETF) by a dishonest broker, giving you the impression that you are investing in Bitcoin while, in fact, you are buying other coins.

In this instance, you are duped into thinking you are investing in Bitcoin while, in reality, you are purchasing other coins, whatever they may be. Given that the returns will differ significantly, this is crucial. For example, the price of Bitcoin might stay essentially constant, providing only moderate gains when compared to alternative cryptocurrencies that performed better.

It can also be the case in reverse. You can be told by a dishonest broker that you are investing in a less costly coin, but, in reality, they are buying Bitcoin. They tidy up, and you receive "modest" reimbursements. Remember that this isn't entirely against the law. Although dishonest, it isn't strictly illegal. Thus, you may maintain an honest relationship with your broker by being aware of the coins, their value, and price changes.

2. Never wager on the farm

This holds for every type of investment. But as recent events have shown, it's simple to get sucked into the excitement around new coinage. ICOs, in particular, frequently experience hype from their issuers. You may be persuaded to pay more for the coins than they are truly worth if you fall victim to the hype. For instance, each currency has a $5 worth. However, you are persuaded to pay twice as much on the grounds that investors will double your share as soon as the coin is released onto the public market.

Investors have been burned in the past when such has occurred. Thus, never risk everything. Research the coin and the underlying technology if you intend to invest in an initial coin offering (ICO). Next, use a comparison to similar ICOs to arrive at a fair market valuation. You can estimate what the coin would be valued if it were to be sold on the open market. You can invest if you believe that similar coins offer sufficient context. However, keep in mind that once an asset is placed on the market, ICOs, like IPOs, can fail. It never makes sense to gamble on the farm because of this.